SATB

Three by Langston

New Moon • Luck • Joy

Text by LANGSTON HUGHES
Music by RICKY IAN GORDON

A RODGERS AND HAMMERSTEIN COMPANY
www.williamsonmusic.com

EXCLUSIVELY DISTRIBUTED BY

New Moon

S. A. T. B. Choir with piano

Text by LANGSTON HUGHES
Music by RICKY IAN GORDON

Copyright ©1998 by Ricky Ian Gordon.
Public Doves Music owner of publication and allied rights throughout the world (administered by Williamson Music).
Text by Langston Hughes Copyright ©1994 by The Estate of Langston Hughes. International Copyright Secured.
ALL RIGHTS RESERVED.

Joy

S. A.T. B. Quartet or Choir with piano

Text by LANGSTON HUGHES
Music by RICKY IAN GORDON

Exuberant and Accented

♩ = 132

f sempre

11

I went to look for joy

Copyright ©1994 by Ricky Ian Gordon.
This arrangement Copyright ©1998 by Ricky Ian Gordon. Public Doves Music owner of publications
and allied rights throughout the world (administered by Williamson Music).
Text by Langston Hughes Copyright ©1959 by Langston Hughes. Copyright renewed 1987 by George
Houston Bass. International Copyright Secured. ALL RIGHTS RESERVED.

WILLIAMSON MUSIC is a registered trademark of the
Family Trust u/w Richard Rodgers, the Family Trust u/w
Dorothy F. Rodgers and the Estate of Oscar Hammerstein II.

0-73999-08951-6

Scan for
pricing &
details